Investigations in English

Tony Bulger

GW00692015

Cassell

Concept, Tony Bulger and Michel Bellity

CASSELL LTD
1 St Anne's Road, Eastbourne
East Sussex BN21 3UN

© Cassell Ltd, 1985

All rights reserved. No part of this publication may be
reproduced, stored in a retrieval system, or transmitted, in any
form or by any means, electronic, mechanical, photocopying,
recording or otherwise, without the prior permission in writing
of the Publishers.

First published 1985

ISBN 0 304 31249 5

Typesetting by Central Southern Typesetters, Eastbourne
Printed in Italy by Tipolitografia G. Canale & C. SpA, Turin

Designed by David Armitage
Illustrations by David Armitage and
Trevor Waugh (pp. 19, 31, 32, 35, 46, 52, 56, 62, 68, 79,
81, 83)
Photographs by Bob Genung and
Martin Mulloy (p. 8) and
by kind permission of The British Tourist Authority (pp. 23, 24,
38, 39, 44, 50, 51, 58, 72, 73)
Cartoon (p.10) by Bill Belcher

Song: *Let's Investigate* . . . © Duncan Lorien, 1984

Contents

Introduction

What is Investigations in English?

Learners who are staying in Britain for a limited period can find that their previous English language instruction is often ill-suited to the demands of the new environment. The walls of the classroom too often hold them back from going out and using English to deepen and expand their knowledge and experience. Investigations in English aims to put the classroom into perspective, to combine previous formal study and practical experience. It tries to promote the notion that using a language is more important than simply learning about it.

How does Investigations in English work?

Investigations in English does not use a traditional language teaching 'method'. There are no formal grammar explanations or exercises. Ten themes are discussed in relation to the learners' own experience of their home environment. Active methods are then developed to relate that experience to that of students in Britain — and the opportunities that this provides to investigate a parallel experience through the practical use of the language.

The classroom is treated as a place to practise the relevant language and to rehearse probable situations. Grammar input is left up to the teacher's perceptions of students' needs. This flexibility makes the book appropriate to different ages and levels of language competence.

Each topic is divided into three sections:

In, Out and **Feedback**

In examines the topic in some detail and provokes students to reflect and draw upon their knowledge of Britain and their home countries. Group exercises are suggested and situations rehearsed. Essential vocabulary is gathered, examined and developed.

Out prepares observation and communication exercises which take place 'on the spot'. There are two main types of activity.

Enquiry and **Mini-Poll**

The ENQUIRY is based on guided observation and note-taking. The MINI-POLL is a group questionnaire which relies on contact with native speakers — friends, the host family, passers-by etc. — to draw up a personal picture of the theme examined.

Feedback is a classroom activity which collates observations and answers and attempts to draw up a general picture of the topic.

It is extremely important to create a record of the work done. Space is allowed in the book for this and an additional record may range from a simple note-book or diary, regularly checked by the teacher, to a file of notes and authentic material collected during the different activities. The actual form will depend on the users. The systematic use of such a record is a vital part of the learning process.

How can Investigations be used?

- The topics may be used in any order and more or less time may be spent on each according to the interests of the class.

- The material provided in each topic section can be expanded upon, depending on the language competence of each student or group.

- The order of presentation corresponds to a simple format:
  —initial contact with the new environment
  —orientation in the new surroundings
  —an investigation of the habits and interests of the people with whom the learners are in contact.

- The exploitation of each unit is left to the teacher and the demands and experience of the learners. The book thus makes demands both on the teacher and on the students to meet this challenge.

- The advantage of the course lies in its flexibility and in an approach which provides opportunities for stimulating and enriching experiences.
  Investigations in English aims to excite interest and encourage exploration.

To the student

Classrooms are like rehearsal rooms: they prepare you for the real performance. Language is not lived in a classroom: it is experienced outside, in the streets, shops and houses, with the people who use it every day.

Like a rehearsal, **Investigations** gives you all you need to prepare yourself. The answers and experiences are not contained in the pages but in what you will do actively in the environment.

So you are not using a traditional language method. We count on two elements to motivate you. First and most important is that you are — or will soon be — in Britain. The second is that you will be here for a limited time: it may be a week, a month or six months, but you have a definite period of stay.

We imagine, too, that you are interested in learning. Not just the language, but about the people who speak it and what they do with it. So, we have chosen ten themes from everyday experience, and have prepared ten investigations for you to carry out. We also give you suggestions for many more follow-up activities to complement what you do.

But be careful: we are asking a lot of you. We want you to make the effort to go out and meet people, to observe and compare without feeling you have to make a judgement. People, habits, institutions are usually different from one's own, not better or worse.

You will, we hope, be staying in a host family. Those people will be your best contact with everyday life. Talk to them, ask their opinions, tell them your own — but remember the British tradition of reserve and privacy. You will have to decide for yourself the best way to go about winning their confidence.

So, if you're prepared to try something different, something challenging, let's go and investigate!

A final word for teachers

The success of the method greatly depends on the collaboration of people outside the classroom. Emphasis should be placed in the early phases of the course on the best ways to approach and involve these people who are not necessarily prepared for such an experience!

Initial reactions are often: "It's asking too much of the students" or "People won't be interested in helping". Our experience has shown that the opposite is true when careful preparations have been made and where the exercises have been made relevant to the previous knowledge and experience of the students and to where they are staying.

The section **Streetwork** shows in a simplified manner how such exercises may be practised in simple and practical situations. The unit contains useful information for day-to-day 'survival' in the new environment.

Acknowledgements

SPECIAL THANKS for the work done by teachers of the British European Centre in applying and developing these active methods and to Brenda Nelson for her invaluable assistance in preparing the manuscript for publication. Thanks also to Dilys Brown for her advice and suggestions.

Streetwork

Introduction
Using **Investigations** means going out and asking questions — in the street, in shops, in the family. In this section, we try to help you ask questions with confidence.

Is it difficult to approach someone in the street and ask questions?
Not if you do it in the right way . . .
Most people will be happy to answer a few questions unless they are in a hurry to get somewhere. When you approach someone, always begin by saying, 'Excuse me,'.

At the beginning, ask questions you know the answers to, just to make sure that you understand — and to build up your confidence.
> *Excuse me . . .*
> *Can you help me?*
> *What time is it, please?*
> *Which bus goes to Burton Road?*
> *Can you tell me where the post office is, please?*

When you begin a conversation, you can say 'May I . . .?'
> *May I ask you some questions, please?*
> *May I talk to you for a few minutes?*

People will be even more helpful if you explain why you are asking questions.

I'm studying English at . . .
I'm interested in the British way of life . . .
My class is finding out about English houses . . .
Our teacher has asked us to get information about what British people usually do in their spare time . . .
This is our book, **Investigations**. *We have to . . .*

Let's look at words which will help you.
Many question words begin with WH–.

What . . .?
What is your name?
What is this called in English?
What is the most popular sport in Britain?

When . . .?
When is the last bus?
When do the shops open?
When do you have dinner?

Notice that 'When' often means 'At what time?'

Which . . .?
Which bus goes to the High Street?
Which do you prefer, tea or coffee?

Where . . .?
Where is the railway station?
Where can I do my laundry?
Where does the 21 bus stop?

. . . and without WH–

Why . . .?
Why do you say 'a request stop'?
Why do banks shut so early?
Why are there so many elderly people here?

How . . .?
How do you spell . . .?
How do I make a reverse charges call?
How can my parents send me money quickly?

Other useful expressions with How . . .?
How much does this cost?
How far is it to the shopping centre?
How old are you?

Don't be afraid to ask people to repeat their answers.
Sorry, could you say that again, please?
I didn't quite catch that. Could you repeat it?
Could you spell that, please?

Always thank people for their help — even if they say they haven't got time to help you!
Thank you very much.
Thanks for your help.
Thank you. That was very interesting/useful/helpful.

Groupwork

Divide into pairs and look at the pictures in this section.
Ask as many questions as you can think of.

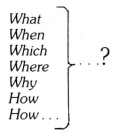

What
When
Which
Where } ...?
Why
How
How ...

One of the first things you will probably have to do is change money. In pairs, work out questions you will have to ask. For example, where to change money . . . when you can do it . . . how much you want to change . . .
Look at the young student below, then practise asking each other further questions.

Think of questions you may want to ask, e.g.
When do British people usually eat in the evening? What is the evening meal called?
Where do British people spend their holidays? How much do you spend on your annual holiday?

Now you go on . . .

When you go out, remember:
Always start with *'Excuse me,'* and finish with *'Thank you'*.
Cars drive on the left!

Good luck.

Investigations
in English

Name _____

Studying at _____

_____

Date _____

Address _____

_____

_____

Tipsheets

Money

Information

- Bank notes used in Britain are:
  £20   £10   £5

  Coins used in Britain are:
  £1   50p   20p   10p   5p   2p   1p (100p = £1)

- Banks are open from 9.30am to 3.30pm, Mondays to Fridays.

Tips

- Don't carry more money than you need.
- Change large notes at banks.
- Try to have the correct change ready when travelling by bus. Only offer coins to bus conductors or drivers.
- Shop-keepers prefer small amounts for small purchases.
- Remember exchange rates can vary so keep some 'emergency' money for the end of your stay in Britain.
- Keep money and travellers cheques in a safe place.

Things to do

- Keep your own Exchange Record
  eg

DATE	Amount changed	Amount received (£)	Amount spent

- Find out at a bank how to have money transferred quickly from your country just in case . . .
- Find out where the nearest bank is:

  _____

  _____

- A few banks are open on Saturday mornings. Is there one near you?

Phone calls

Information

- In an emergency, dial 999 and ask for the service you want   Fire
                                                       Police
         Ambulance

It is not necessary to pay for emergency calls.
- There are several different types of pay phone in Britain. In a phone booth, read the dialling instructions carefully and check you have the coins you need.
- You can make a reverse charges call without putting any money in.
- It is cheaper to make phone calls between 6pm and 8am (Mon–Fri) and at the weekend.

Tips

- If you are staying with a family, always ask before using the phone and offer to pay for the call.
- The family will probably allow you to call home if you reverse the charges.
- If you answer the phone, give the number.

Don't be afraid to ask callers to repeat what they said if you don't understand! eg I'm sorry, I didn't catch what you said. Could you say it again?
- Don't try to call abroad from an ordinary public phone box.

Things to do

- Find out where the nearest phone box is _____

  _____

- Find out where the nearest international phone box is.
- Write down the direct dialling code for your own country.

International Code	Country Code	Area Code	(Number)
010	_____	_____	_____

- Write down the operator number for calls to your country. _____
- Find out what information services are available and write down some of the numbers.

  eg Tourist information _____   Speaking Clock _____

Health

Information

- If you feel ill you can go and see a doctor (a GP — General Practitioner).
- There are NHS (National Health Service) doctors and private doctors in Britain. Charges made by NHS doctors will generally be lower. Visitors from some countries can receive free medical treatment (eg EEC Countries).
- If your doctor decides you need medicine, he will give you a prescription which you must take to a chemist's. You will have to pay a charge for each item.

Tips

- If you suffer from any medical condition, tell your host family and the school when you arrive.
- If you feel ill while you are here, tell somebody immediately.

Things to do

- Find out the name and address of your family's local GP and/or the school doctor.

  _____

  _____

- Make a note of a chemist's near your home or school.

Tipping

Information

- If you use some services in Britain you will be expected to give a tip, eg taxis — for a very short journey, minimum tip — 20p. For longer journeys 10–20 per cent of fare.
  Other people who might expect a tip are:
  — Hairdressers
  — Luggage porters
  — Hotel staff.
- You don't give tips in pubs.
- In some restaurants a tip will be expected because service is not included in the bill. The tip should be approximately 10% of the cost of the meal. In other restaurants, if service *is* included in the bill, a tip is not necessary.

Living with a family

Tips

- It is a good idea to ask your host family about the 'Rules of the House' when you first arrive. Customs vary from country to country and behaviour which is perfectly normal in one country may be considered rude, shocking, strange or unacceptable in another! eg the cost of hot water may regulate how often people have a bath or a shower . . .

Things to do

- Find out:
  — if you can have a key
  — when meals are served
  — when you can use the bathroom
  — when you are expected to be home at night
  — if you can use the TV, stereo etc.
  — if you can invite friends home

  — _____

Homes

There are 4 people in the Cook family. This is their house. It's 23 Anglesea Road. The area of the town is called North End. The house also has a name: it is called the Nuthatch. There is a small garden in front and a back yard and the house is next to a block of flats.

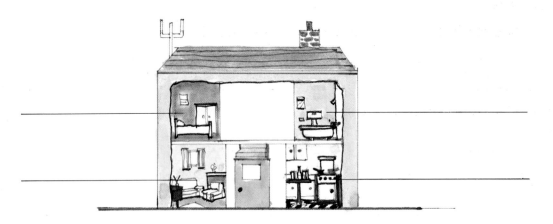

Label the diagram.

What are the different rooms used for?

In which room do you:

◊ do the washing up? _____

◊ eat breakfast? _____

◊ watch television? _____

What are these?

_____   _____   _____

Linklist

This is a Linklist. It helps you to compare things in Britain and in your own country; it will make you think about both at the same time.

In the classroom, ask your teacher and other students to help you fill in some of the blanks. Later, ask your host family and friends to give you some ideas. When you have finished your Linklist, you can also compare it with those of your classmates. If you are from the same country you may have different ideas or, if you choose someone from another country, you will learn even more!

The subject of this Linklist is homes and the way people live.

In Britain . . .	In my country . . .
◊ Most families live in houses, not flats.	◊
◊ Most houses have gardens, even in cities.	◊
◊ Most houses are semi-detached.	◊
◊ Some houses have names as well as numbers.	◊
◊ Many streets look the same.	◊
◊	◊
◊	◊
◊	◊

Groupwork

This is to help you practise asking questions.

Look at this checklist from a market research company. Think of other questions you would like to ask.

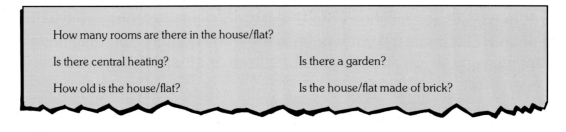

How many rooms are there in the house/flat?

Is there central heating?   Is there a garden?

How old is the house/flat?   Is the house/flat made of brick?

_____

_____

_____

_____

_____

Now choose a partner and ask the questions you have worked out. Talk about your own home and your host family's. Change partners and move around the class.

Read the following advertisements.

Which would you prefer to live in?
Are they typical English houses?

1930s semi
2 reception, 4 bed, bath with shower
separate wc
rewired throughout
gas central heating
garage
large rear garden

immaculate spacious, second-floor flat
2 double bedrooms
large kitchen/diner
use of communal garden

2-bed terraced house
fully modernised throughout
through lounge/diner
close to all amenities, excellent
bus service to town centre

Read this description:

> Mr and Mrs Ponsonby Smythe live in a large mansion in Surrey. They have ten bedrooms, eight guestrooms with private bathrooms and dressing rooms. There are two living rooms, a dining room, a games room, a smoking room, a kitchen, a pantry and a wine cellar. Their staff of six servants live in two cottages nearby.

Would you like to live in a house like this?
What is your ideal house?

Words

Check that you understand this vocabulary. You have probably used some of the words in the first part of the unit. See how many you know.

to live in a house/a flat/a bungalow
to have central heating/double-glazing/roof insulation

The design and layout of a house are important.
Some have a separate dining room and living room.
Others are more open-plan.
Some have built-in wardrobes, cupboards and shelving.
Do-it-yourself (DIY) is now very popular: many people decorate/repair/renovate their own houses.

Write down any extra vocabulary below:

Listening

If you have time, listen to what these people have to say about 'Homes'.

◊ A Councillor _____

◊ Mr Williams, aged 32 _____

◊ An Architect _____

◊ An Estate Agent _____

Ready?

You have practised asking questions inside the classroom, now we want you to get more information by asking your host family some questions.

First of all, show them what you did in class and ask their opinion. Then ask them some more detailed questions.

Steady . . .

As a class, suggest questions that might be useful for obtaining information. Your teacher will write them up on the board. When you have about twenty questions, choose about ten and write them down following the pattern below. This is a 'Mini-Poll'.

Go!

'May I ask you a few questions, please?'

MINI-POLL

i   Is your house *(a)* detached? *(b)* semi-detached? *(c)* terraced?

ii   Do you have *(a)* a front garden? *(b)* a back garden? *(c)* neither?

iii   Do you prefer to live *(a)* in a big city? *(b)* in a suburb? *(c)* in the country?

iv   Which do you prefer? *(a)* A house. *(b)* A flat. *(c)* It doesn't matter which.

v   Do you find English homes *(a)* very comfortable? *(b)* fairly comfortable? *(c)* too small?

Now you carry on . . .

_____

_____

_____

_____

_____

_____

_____

_____

Feedback

Here are the results of the Mini-Poll answered by Mr and Mrs Anwell in Portsmouth:

1. Our house is seventy years old.
2. It is a Victorian terraced house.
3. We would never live in a flat.
4. We like living in a suburb; we are near everything except the noise.
5. English people really make a house feel like home.
6. We don't have central heating. We only heat two rooms.
7. There is a small garden at the back; we would like a bigger one.
8. Our son and daughter-in-law live very close. We babysit for them.
9. I don't think all the houses in England look the same. Each is different.
10. I don't think we will move house again.

How do these answers compare with what you found out?

Choose a partner and compare answers. Report your findings to the class.

Look at the report below. Write a similar one using the information you have collected.

I have found that most English people live in houses with small gardens. They park their cars outside in the street. A lot of houses are made of brick. They are built in long straight rows.   PTO →

_____
_____
_____
_____
_____
_____
_____
_____
_____
_____
_____

Things to do

◊ Draw a picture and a plan of your host family's house and send it to your parents.

◊ Swap addresses of host families with your classmates so they know where you live.

◊ Walk down a quiet street and note down all the different names that you see on houses. Which is the prettiest? Which is the funniest?

◊ Look at the names of the streets around you where you are staying. Do the names mean anything to you? Ask people who live there to explain where the names come from. See if they know!

◊ To practise asking questions of people you do not know, walk up to someone and ask him or her to explain how to get to your host family's house, or to the school. You will find that it is easier than you think!

Towns

This is Newtown. It's a town — it's bigger than a village and smaller than a city. Newtown is quite small but there is a lot to discover.

Where would you:

◊ get tourist information? _____

◊ get information about buses? _____

◊ buy presents for your family? _____

◊ go if you were ill? _____

What are these?

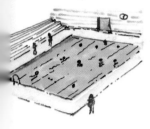    

_____ _____ _____ _____ _____

Linklist

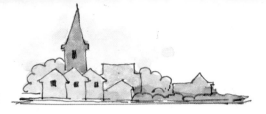

The subject of this Linklist is cities, towns and villages. Add to it as you gather information and form opinions.

In Britain . . .	In my country . . .
◊ A city must have a cathedral.	◊
◊ There are 12 counties and each county has a major town.	◊
◊ Seaside towns are popular as retirement places.	◊
◊ London is the capital.	◊
◊	◊
◊	◊
◊	◊
◊	◊
◊	◊
◊	◊
	◊
	◊

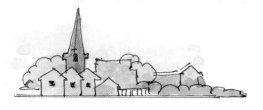

Groupwork

Choose a partner. One covers up the left-hand map below and the other covers up the right-hand one. Exchange information so that you can complete your maps.

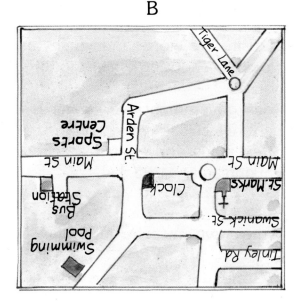

A

B

ask about:
St. Mark's Church
the swimming pool
the sports centre
the bus station

the police station
the shopping area
the bowling alley
the railway station
ask about:

Check and compare. Choose a partner, someone from a different country if possible. What are the major differences between British towns and towns in your country? Discuss these together.

What is the first thing you notice? Look out of the window and look for a minute at what is around you. Listen carefully. What seems different?

Read this description of Hightown and compare it with the town you are living in at the moment.

> The town is small and clean. Many buildings are made of red brick and there are a few grey concrete office buildings. There are lots of little shops and one supermarket. There are red pillar-boxes and phone boxes everywhere. There are no cinemas or theatres. There is a disco and four pubs.

Words

Check that you understand this vocabulary.

Town maps usually show shopping areas/industrial areas/residential areas.
Shops — department store/shopping centre/pedestrian precinct/corner shops.
Industry — factories/industrial estate/warehouses.
Houses — housing estate/modern building/Victorian/Edwardian-style houses.
Local government — civic offices, Town Hall, guildhall.
Leisure facilities — tennis courts, swimming pool, golf course.
Street plan — one-way streets, roundabouts, traffic lights, road junctions, No Parking areas, cycle paths.

Write down any extra vocabulary below:

Listening

If you have time, listen to what these people have to say about 'Towns'.

◊ A Newcomer _____

◊ Peter Hanson, aged 17 _____

◊ A Local Businessman _____

◊ Harold Clark, aged 73 _____

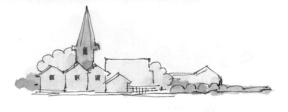

Out

Ready?

We are going to do an Enquiry on the town or city where you are staying. The aim is to make a detailed map of the town.

First of all, divide into groups of three.

Here are some different areas of Enquiry:

TRANSPORT: Where are the most useful bus stops? What are the major routes? Is there a way of paying less if you take a bus regularly? How often do buses run from the centre? What time is the last bus in the evening? Are there other ways of travelling around town?

SHOPS: Where are the shopping areas? Where can you find shops for clothes, sports goods, food, writing paper? What time do shops open and shut? Are they open on Saturday and Sunday?

ENTERTAINMENT & FACILITIES: Where are the swimming pools . . . cinemas . . . parks and gardens . . . libraries . . . discos . . . cafés . . . information centre . . . hospitals . . . theatres . . . sports facilities?

Steady . . .

Each group should select one section. This is an ideal way to ask people you meet in the street very simple questions. You can also ask people in shops and information offices.

Go!

Off you go into town.

Feedback

Here is a sample of the results of an Enquiry carried out by one group of students. Do the same for your town. First, copy down a skeleton map. Then, in your groups, go and share information with each other.

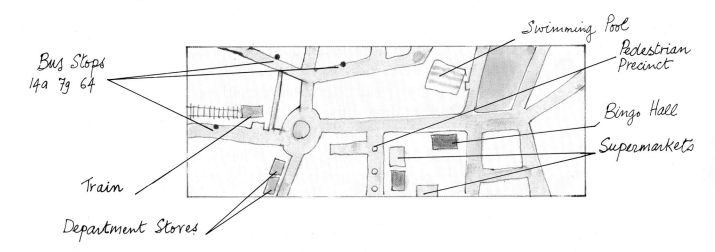

Bus Stops
14a 7g 64

Swimming Pool

Pedestrian Precinct

Bingo Hall

Supermarkets

Train

Department Stores

Things to do

◊ Work out what the name of your town means.
Here are some notes to help you:
-ham: a homestead
-by: a farm or village
-stead: a religious site
-chester: a Roman camp
-ing: groups of people

◊ Ask your teacher to help you with any others.

◊ Find the crest of your town and its motto and copy it into your book.

◊ Find the name of the town with which your host-city is twinned. Do you know that town? Why do you think the two towns were twinned?

◊ On the noticeboard in your classroom, pin a detailed map of the town. Mark on it where everyone in the class is living. Write down the name of their host family and the 'phone number.

Television

 Here are the 4 channels you can watch on British television. Do you know any of them? Which one does your host family watch the most often? People watch a lot of television in England!

Can you answer these questions?

◊ At what time is the main evening news on each channel? _____

◊ What kind of programmes are shown during the day? _____

◊ What kind of programme is 'Coronation Street'? _____

◊ What sort of programmes are shown on BBC 2? _____

◊ What is the ITV channel in your area? _____

◊ Do all the channels have advertising? _____

◊ Where do you find out what programmes are on television? _____

If you can't answer these questions, ask your friends in class and then your teacher.

Write down some of the programmes you have watched since you came to Britain.

_____

_____

_____

_____

Linklist

The subject of this Linklist is television and what people think of television.

Add to it as usual.

In Britain . . .	In my country . . .
◊ Advertisements appear in the middle of programmes and between them.	◊
◊ Programmes finish at about 12.00pm. *not now*	◊
◊ Breakfast television is quite popular.	◊
◊ There are 4 channels — 2 BBC and 2 independent. *more now*	◊
◊ Children's programmes are mainly shown between 4 pm and 5 pm.	◊
◊ *Same* Many families rent their TV set.	◊
◊	◊
◊	◊
◊	◊
◊	◊
◊	

Groupwork

Here's what a famous journalist said about England:

> The first thing you notice is that the coins are heavier, the buildings are redder, the grass is greener, the people are quieter, the manners are better, the food is worse. You notice brick buildings, streets that look the same, red pillarboxes — and a lot of other things that make up your impression of England.

Imagine you are a journalist for your country's TV network: you are going to make a short documentary on England. Work with two other journalists. You must decide what things you will show and what will be the theme of your report.

* Write down the story scene by scene.
* Now go round to the other groups and see how your ideas are different or similar.
* Finally, make up a class documentary.

_____

_____

_____

_____

_____

_____

Words

Check that you understand this vocabulary.

On a TV set you can change the channel/switch over. You can adjust the sound/the colour/the brightness/the contrast.

Independent television is funded by money from advertisements/commercials; BBC by the TV licence fee.

Programmes include talk shows, soap operas, drama, sport, comedies . . . If you are interested in current affairs, watch the news and documentaries.

Write down any extra vocabulary below:

Listening

If you have time, listen to what these people have to say about 'Television'.

◊ A Primary School Teacher _____

◊ A Secondary School Pupil, aged 12 _____

◊ A Politician _____

◊ A Young Viewer _____

 **Ready?**

Have you watched much television? It is probably rather difficult to understand, but look at the variety of programmes; look at the advertisements — sometimes called 'commercials' — and find out as much as you can by observing. Are there lots of commercials for tea and coffee, for frozen food, for holidays abroad, for headache pills?

Let's find out a little more about what the English think of their television. We'll use the questionnaire method.

Steady . . .

As a class, discuss with your teacher what you want to know. Write down the questions and ask your host family to help you answer them.

Go!

'May I ask you a few questions, please?'

MINI-POLL

> i   Do you watch television for *(a)* 2 hours a day or less? *(b)* 4 hours a day or less? *(c)* more than 4 hours a day?
>
> ii   Do you prefer *(a)* light entertainment? *(b)* current affairs programmes? *(c)* serials and dramas?
>
> iii   Which channel do you watch most often? *(a)* BBC 1. *(b)* BBC 2. *(c)* ITV. *(d)* Channel 4.
>
> iv   Do you think that commercials are *(a)* unnecessary? *(b)* necessary but annoying? *(c)* entertaining?
>
> v   What is there too much of? *(a)* Soap operas. *(b)* Documentaries. *(c)* Comedy shows. *(d)* American series.
>
> Now you carry on . . .
>
> _____
>
> _____
>
> _____
>
> _____
>
> _____

Feedback

Here are the answers given by Mr & Mrs Stenning in Bournemouth to their guest's questions:

1 We always watch BBC because we don't like commercials.
2 We like documentaries, the news and serious programmes.
3 We only watch about 2 hours a day.
4 We have a colour TV set and a video recorder.
5 There is great variety on British TV. It is the best in Europe.
6 There are too many American series and too much violence.
7 Children watch too much TV.
8 We hate 'Coronation Street' and programmes like that.
9 Breakfast TV is a bad idea.

What questions did the student ask the Stennings? Are these answers similar to the ones you obtained?

Compare your answers with a partner's. Now both of you check with other pairs.

Report back to the class.

◊ What does the class think of British TV?

◊ What do the host families think of British TV?

◊ Which was the most popular channel?

◊ Which was the most popular programme?

Game

In two teams, take it in turns to mime the titles of any TV programmes that you know. The other team must guess the programme. You have 2 minutes to do the mime; the other team has 3 minutes to guess. One point for every correct answer.

Things to do

◊ Buy the *Radio Times* and the *TV Times* as souvenirs.

◊ Find out how much a licence costs for a black-and-white TV and for a colour TV. Is there a licence for a video recorder?

◊ Find out the name of your local ITV station.

◊ Make a list of the kinds of commercials you see in an evening.

◊ Watch a whole programme from beginning to end!

Shopping

This is a town High Street with its different shops. Does it look like the town you are staying in? In many towns, a lot of small shops like these have been replaced by supermarkets and department stores.

What do the following shops sell?

◊ Boots   _____

◊ W H Smith   _____

◊ C & A   _____

◊ Marks & Spencer   _____

Where in this town can you buy:

◊ a street map?   _____

◊ postcards and writing paper?   _____

◊ tennis balls?   _____

◊ a pullover?   _____

◊ presents?   _____

Are there shops which sell products from your country?

What do they sell?

Write down some things that you have bought
in England.   _____

_____

Linklist

The subject of this Linklist is shops and shopping. Add to it as usual.

In Britain . . .	In my country . . .
◊ Most shops open at 9 and close at 5.30.	◊
◊ Most shops are closed on Sunday.	◊
◊ There is a minimum age for buying cigarettes.	◊
◊ Most people shop for food in supermarkets.	◊
◊ VAT is 15%.	◊
◊	◊
◊	◊
◊	◊
◊	◊

Groupwork

Are there any differences between shops here and shops in your own country?

With other students of the same nationality, imagine that you are going to set up a 'typical' French, Italian, Spanish or other shop here in England. What type of shop would it be? What would you call it? What products would you sell?

Draw a picture of the front and a plan of the inside.

Read this extract from a tourist brochure about a shop called *La Casa de Inghilterra* in Brescia, Italy.

> The shop is very quiet inside and everybody talks in whispers. The floors are wooden and the smell of coffee, tea and wool is very strong. All the customers stand in polite queues and are served by smiling shop assistants in morning suits. You can buy tea, cakes, jams, coffee, sweets, bacon, pullovers and many other English products.

Do you know any shop like this in England? Where is it? Ask an English person to describe Harrods or Fortnum & Mason's to you.

Game

Play with a partner. He or she is a shopkeeper and will choose what sort of shop it is without telling you. You must try to find out what kind of shop it is by asking:

'Do you sell . . .?' or 'Do you stock . . .?'

When you have found out the answer, change places.

Words

Check that you understand this vocabulary.

to go shopping for food/clothes/presents
to compare prices/to look for a bargain
to be served by a shop assistant
self-service/wire basket/supermarket trolley
a packet of . . ./a box of . . ./a carton of . . ./a tin of . . . etc.
Goods can be displayed on hangers/on a counter/on open shelves.
Products can be exclusive to one shop — with their own brand name — or generally available.

In a shop:
Remember you don't have to buy. You can always say — 'I'm just looking, thank you.'

Write down any extra vocabulary below:

Listening

If you have time, listen to what these people have to say about 'Shopping'.

◊ A Shopkeeper _____

◊ A Lady Shopper _____

◊ A Department Store Manager _____

◊ A Sub-Post Mistress, aged 67 _____

◀ Out

Ready?
Our enquiry today is about the different shops, goods and prices in the town you are staying in or visiting. Here's a shopping basket and a list:

meat
fish
eggs
milk
bread and cakes
tea and coffee
shoe polish
45 rpm single
postcards
tennis racket
paperback book
sticking plasters
pens
soap

Divide the list up into different headings.
Now, in groups, choose a category.
Your Enquiry is to check at different shops and to take note of selection, prices, display and so on.

Steady . . .
In the shops, take your time and observe closely. Don't hesitate to ask people for information. When you walk into a shop, stop for a moment and notice the different sounds and smells. What sort of music do they play in supermarkets?

Go!
Off we go. Remember to explain what you are doing: shopkeepers are worried when they see a group of people in their shop who are not buying. Show them this book if necessary. Make your notes but try not to get in the way!

Feedback

Here are two reports from teams in Poole. One team was looking at meat and vegetables and the other at leisure goods. This is what they had to say:

> We looked at 4 shops. The butcher's shops were like those in France except the cuts of meat were different. There were more frozen foods on sale. The choice of vegetables was not very wide but most of it was grown in England (except for Dutch tomatoes). The presentation was not very imaginative. The people were not allowed to touch the fruit.

> What a selection! Video games, computers, electronic games, pocket TVs — some of the things you can't find in our countries yet. The goods were also much cheaper — the shopkeeper told us that VAT was only 15%. Obviously, English people spend a lot of time at home playing with their TVs.

In your report give details of what you saw, who you spoke to and what you discovered.

Now, let's make up a Best Buys Guide from your information. You probably won't want to buy meat but what about a Shetland pullover or an electronic pocket game? A tennis racquet? Something for your host family? Make up a Guide like this:

CLOTHES	<u>William's (High St)</u> Old-fashioned and expensive but has nice sweaters. <u>The Boutique (Market St)</u> Great jeans and T-shirts. Lots of imports. Fairly dear. <u>Marks and Spencer (Will St)</u> Good quality. Reasonable prices. Too crowded at the weekend.
LEISURE	<u>Marples (North St)</u> Wide selection of magazines & books. Pocket video games at low prices. <u>Hamways (East St)</u> Good for presents. 'typically English'

_____

_____

_____

_____

_____

_____

_____

Things to do

◊ Make up a list of presents to take home with you.

◊ Think of one item you will miss when you go back.

◊ Think of one item you will be glad to find when you go back.

◊ Cut out any adverts for shops, sales, special offers and so on from your local paper.

Meals

 Here are the main meals of the day.
Is this what you eat?
What do you drink with your meals?

Ask another student:

◊ What time are the meals in your host family? _____

◊ Do the family all eat together? _____

◊ How many courses do you eat? _____

◊ What do you say when you begin to eat? _____

   when you have finished? _____

Write down a typical day's menu in your host family.

Breakfast	Lunch	Evening Meal
_____	_____	_____
_____	_____	_____
_____	_____	_____
_____	_____	_____
_____	_____	_____

Linklist

The subject of this Linklist is food, meals and people's attitudes to food.
Add to it as usual.

In Britain . . .	In my country . . .
◊ Everyone drinks a lot of tea.	◊
◊ Frozen and tinned food are very popular.	◊
◊ Many people eat large breakfasts.	◊
◊ Milk is delivered every day	◊
◊	◊
◊	◊
◊	◊
◊	◊
◊	
◊	

Groupwork

What are the main differences between meals in England and meals in your country? Choose a partner (if possible from another country) and compare notes.

Discussion

The Victorian Era was very strict. Here is a list of instructions given to young men about how to behave at table:

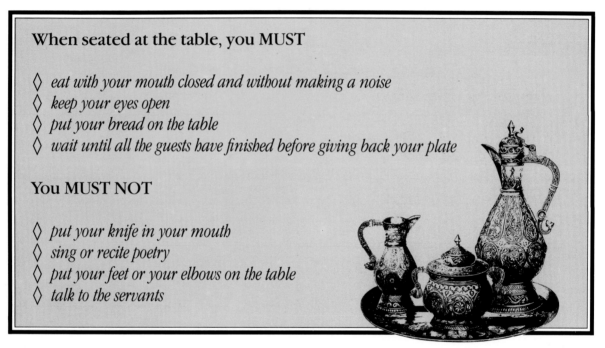

When seated at the table, you MUST

◊ *eat with your mouth closed and without making a noise*
◊ *keep your eyes open*
◊ *put your bread on the table*
◊ *wait until all the guests have finished before giving back your plate*

You MUST NOT

◊ *put your knife in your mouth*
◊ *sing or recite poetry*
◊ *put your feet or your elbows on the table*
◊ *talk to the servants*

Times have changed . . . or have they?
What are the rules today? Discuss this with your class then write a letter to a friend to tell him or her what they should do in England.

Words

Check that you understand this vocabulary.
take-away/convenience/'junk'/fast food
food can be fresh/frozen/tinned
it can be fried/baked/grilled

to cook/prepare a meal
A recipe includes a list of ingredients

Write down any extra vocabulary below:

Listening

If you have time, listen to what these people have to say about 'Meals'.

◊ A Businessman _____

◊ A Teacher _____

◊ A Northerner living in the South _____

◊ Helen Jones, aged 42 _____

Out

Ready?

We are going to find out more about eating habits in Britain. Draw up a list of questions which you can ask your host family.

Steady . . .

Discuss the subject with your class before choosing the final list of questions.

Go!

'May I ask you a few questions, please?'

MINI-POLL

i   What would you eat on a special occasion? *(a)* Steak. *(b)* Scampi. *(c)* Curry. *(d)* Something else.

ii   Which do you prefer? *(a)* Going to a restaurant. *(b)* Eating at home.

iii   What is a typically English dish? *(a)* Bacon and eggs. *(b)* Shepherd's pie. *(c)* Steak and kidney pie. *(d)* Something else.

iv   What is the most important meal of the day? *(a)* Breakfast. *(b)* Lunch. *(c)* Tea.

v   Which 'foreign' food do you enjoy? *(a)* Italian. *(b)* Indian. *(c)* Chinese. *(d)* French.

Now you carry on . . .

_____

_____

_____

_____

_____

_____

_____

_____

_____

_____

Feedback

Here are the answers given by Mr & Mrs Williams in Brighton:

1 We don't often go to restaurants.
2 We eat three meals a day; breakfast is the most important.
3 We eat as a family.
4 I don't like garlic or spicy food (Mr Williams). I don't like garlic (Mrs).
5 For a special meal, I cook steak and bake a cake.
6 We drink water with our meals.
7 My children like crisps, sweets and 'junk' food.
8 We never drink wine. I like tea and my husband drinks beer.
9 I like Greek food but I never cook it.
10 I like sliced white bread.

Do you find any similarities between these responses and yours? Work out what questions the students asked.

Choose a partner and compare your two sets of answers, then make a report to the class. What does the class now know about people in Britain?

◊ Do they eat regular meals as a family?

◊ Do they often go out to restaurants?

◊ What kinds of food are most popular?

◊ Are there some foods that are common in your country but never eaten in Britain?

Write down all your conclusions.

_____

_____

_____

_____

_____

Things to do

◊ Take a photograph of your favourite dish.

◊ Ask your host family for a typically English recipe — try taking it by dictation!

◊ With your classmates, make up a list of your most favourite and your least favourite meals.

Travelling

Here are some ways of travelling around Britain. Which is the fastest? Which is the most comfortable? What is the best way to travel if you want to see a new country?

Are you used to the traffic being on the 'wrong' side of the road in Britain? What else do you know?

◊ Where do you see FARE STAGE? What does it mean? _____

◊ What is a REQUEST STOP? What must you do there? _____

◊ Which is cheaper for long-distance travel — train or coach? _____

◊ What is an AWAYDAY? _____

◊ What do these symbols represent?   _____

What about the place where you are staying:

Write down the major bus routes and their numbers. _____

Which bus do you take home? to the town centre? _____

Linklist

The subject of this Linklist is types of transport and methods of travelling. Add to it as usual.

In Britain . . .	In my country . . .
◊ There is an underground in several cities.	◊
◊ Some buses have drivers and conductors.	◊
◊ The railways are government-run and called BRITISH RAIL.	◊
◊ Travelling on the motorways is free.	◊
◊ There are A-roads, B-roads and motorways (M).	◊
◊	◊
◊	◊
◊	◊
◊	◊
	◊
	◊

Groupwork

Are the English good drivers? What about people in your country? Be honest!

There are too many cars on the road! Cities are blocked with traffic. Listen to this poor student:

> I was late for school yesterday because I took the bus during the rush hour. First, the traffic lights failed. Then a lorry had an accident just in front of us. The cars could not move. Drivers were walking over the roofs of their cars to get to telephones. The jam lasted for two hours!

The traffic problem must be solved.
Choose a partner. You are both famous urban planners.
Choose a name for your firm.

Here is the city of Portsmouth, which for years has had a plan to close the 'island' part of the city to all traffic.

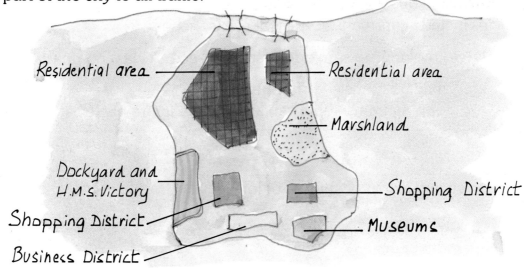

Your budget is £4 million. Look at the layout of the 'island' area and the list of costs:

Construction costs
Car park for 2000: £1 million
Car park for 4000: £1.5 million
Train lines: £400 per mile
Road (2 lane): £200 per mile
Underground: £500 per mile

Vehicles
Bus for 50 passengers: £20,000
Minibus for 20 people: £4,000
Shuttle train: £60,000
Underground
    (train + 10 carriages): £2m.

Your firm must find the best solution to the problem within the budget. Remember you have to ban all cars and service all areas. Where would you place your car parks? Remember that building an underground system is much more disruptive than building a road.

When you have finished, compare your ideas with those of other firms then compile a class plan. Send it to the local Council!

Does any form of transport get special encouragement from the government in your country? — e.g. road/rail/canal/air.

Is there a subsidy for passenger travel or for goods?

Do local people complain when a new motorway or airport is built?

Words

Check that you understand this vocabulary.

In towns, car-drivers need to look out for one-way streets, pedestrian precincts, traffic lights, pelican and zebra crossings, double-yellow lines, bus lanes, roundabouts . . .

to travel by train/by bus/by car
to catch/miss a bus
Vehicles include cars, vans, lorries, buses, coaches.

Trains have smoking/no smoking/first class/second class compartments.

Passengers may be tourists/commuters.
There are stopping trains/suburban lines/InterCity trains/125s.

Write down any extra vocabulary below:

Listening

If you have time, listen to what these people have to say about 'Travelling'.

◊ A Bus Driver _____

◊ A Passenger _____

◊ A Councillor _____

◊ A Member of a Watchdog Committee _____

Out

Ready?

We are going to do two things in today's Enquiry:
  i   a traffic survey.
  ii get information about buses and trains.

Steady . . .

For the traffic survey —
Divide into groups of three. Your teacher will assign each group to a different part of town. Copy this survey chart:

BRITISH-BUILT CAR		FOREIGN-BUILT CAR		LORRY	BUS	OTHER
Over 5 years old	Under 5	Over 5 years old	Under 5			

Put a stroke for every vehicle that goes by, and make up sets like this: ~~HH~~T (= 5)
Your teacher will tell you how you know if a car is over or under 5 years old.

For the second part of the Enquiry —
The class should now divide into two groups.

Group 1: Find out where the main bus station is; what the number to dial for information is; what time the first and last buses to the centre of town are; what the major routes are.

Group 2: Find out where the railway station is (or if there is more than one); what cities are served directly; which local lines take you to places of interest.

Choose a partner and practise asking for information.

Go!

Let's go. Remember: In Britain, cars drive on the left. Be very careful.

Feedback
Let's share our information. Look at this map.

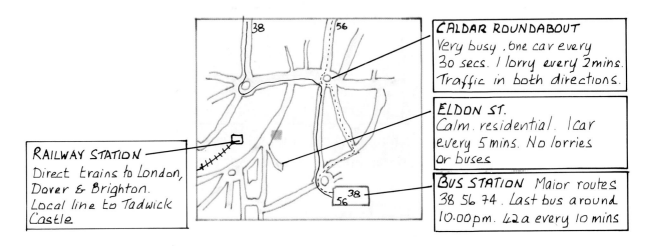

CALDAR ROUNDABOUT
Very busy, one car every
30 secs. 1 lorry every 2mins.
Traffic in both directions.

ELDON ST.
Calm. residential. 1 car
every 5mins. No lorries
or buses

BUS STATION Major routes
38 56 74. Last bus around
10.00pm. 42a every 10 mins

RAILWAY STATION
Direct trains to London,
Dover & Brighton.
Local line to Tadwick
Castle

Do the same thing for your town. Elect two 'planners' who will transfer the information from the groups to a map on the board. Deal with part 1 and part 2 of the Enquiry separately.

Have you discovered any transport problems? If the problem is serious enough, suggest a solution and send a letter to the local paper.

Things to do

◊ Take a photograph of a double-decker bus.

◊ Write to your parents, explaining to them how to get from the nearest Channel port to your host family's house.

◊ Start a collection of different tickets from the bus, the train, the underground, etc. When you look at them six months later, they will remind you of your time in Britain.

◊ Go to the bus or railway station and ask for information about cheap fares and season tickets. If you discover anything interesting, share it with the class.

Holidays

Traditionally English people spend their holidays at the seaside. More people are going abroad now — perhaps to your country — but many still prefer seaside resorts such as Brighton, Bournemouth, Eastbourne or Blackpool.

Can you answer these questions? (Look at a map of Britain.)

◊ Where are the main holiday places? _____

◊ What is the furthest distance of any point from the sea? _____

◊ Are there any mountains in Britain? _____

◊ Where is the Lake District? _____

Here are some tourist attractions.

The Blackpool Tower   Windsor   Stonehenge

Do you know these places?

Can you think of any more?

What are the tourist attractions in or near where you are staying? Write them down:

_____

_____

_____

_____

Linklist

The subject of this Linklist is holidays and the way people like to spend their holidays. Add to it as usual.

In Britain . . .	In my country . . .
◊ People usually have 4 weeks paid holiday a year.	◊
◊ There are 8 public holidays.	◊
◊ ⅓ of the population remains in Britain for their holidays.	◊
◊ The seaside is the most popular type of holiday.	◊
◊ 13½ million overseas tourists visit Britain each year.	◊
◊ Many people have 2 holidays — the main one abroad, and a shorter one in Britain.	◊
◊	◊
◊	◊
◊	◊
◊	◊
◊	◊

Groupwork

How do you spend *your* holidays?

What is your favourite kind of holiday? — beach & swimming?
— sporting & energetic?
— lazy & with the family?
— what else?

How far ahead do you plan a holiday? — a year?
— 6 months?
— a few months?
— a few days?

Imagine you are a travel agent and you have to make up your brochure for this year. Try and make it as exciting as possible because competition is fierce. Choose a partner.

Look at the lists below. Choose 4 or 5 activities then match them up with a different place to do each of them. Next choose your prices — how many days are you offering; is the accommodation in a hotel, a caravan, or at a camp-site? Remember you must cover your costs *and* make a profit.

ACTIVITY	LOCATION	COST
★ Mountaineering	★ Stratford-on-Avon	£200
★ Swimming & sunbathing	★ The Brecon Beacons	£50
★ Hiking & trekking	★ Ben Nevis	£100
★ Camping	★ Blackpool	£180
★ Eating	★ Cornish Riviera	£85
★ Sailing & boating	★ The North York Moors	£120
★ Riding	★ London	?
★ Deep sea diving	★ Dartmoor	?
★ Painting	★ Norfolk Broads	?
★ Karate	★ The Lake District	
★ Ski-ing	★ Loch Ness	
★ Theatres	★ Snowdonia	

When you have finished your brochure, let your teacher choose which 'travel agency' has the most interesting selection of holidays with the best prices. Look and see what other groups have done.

Words

Check that you understand this vocabulary.

to plan/book/enjoy a holiday
to go on holiday
to go sailing/swimming/walking/sight-seeing
to go abroad/on a package holiday/to the seaside/to the countryside

to stay at a hotel/in a caravan/at a youth hostel/at a camp-site
to fly/to hire a car/to travel by coach, train, boat
to pack your clothes in a suitcase/a rucksack

Going on holiday means a change of routine for most people — some want to relax, others like an active holiday.

Write down any extra vocabulary below:

Listening

If you have time, listen to what these people have to say about 'Holidays'.

◊ Mrs Rodgers, aged 47 _____

◊ Malcolm D'Arcy, aged 32 _____

◊ A Travel Agent _____

◊ Diego Vergara _____

Out

Ready?
We are going to ask your host families about their holidays, where they go and what they do.

Discuss the possible questions with your teacher. What do we want to know? What is it polite to ask?

Steady . . .
When all the ideas have been heard, choose a final list of questions and write them down.

Go!

'May I ask you a few questions, please?'

MINI-POLL

i   How many weeks holiday do you have each year? *(a)* 2–3 weeks. *(b)* 3–4 weeks. *(c)* more.

ii   For your main holiday, do you usually *(a)* go abroad? *(b)* stay in Britain?

iii   Do you prefer *(a)* the seaside? *(b)* the countryside. *(c)* a town or a city? *(d)* staying at home?

iv   Do you take your holidays *(a)* all at once? *(b)* spread out over the year?

v   Which continent would you most like to visit (or re-visit)? *(a)* Europe. *(b)* Africa. *(c)* America.

Now you carry on . . .

Feedback

Here are the answers of Mr and Mrs Bolton of Gosport:

1 We always go to Brighton for the month of August.
2 My husband has four weeks' holiday, I have eight (I'm a teacher).
3 We took a package holiday to Spain last year.
4 We want to go to France, to Greece and to the U.S.A.
5 The most beautiful region of Britain that we know is the Lake District.
6 We don't stay in hotels; we stay on camp-sites.
7 For relaxation, we like swimming and reading.
8 We never go to Scotland.
9 We would like to visit somewhere exotic one day.
10 We like being tourists.

What questions did the students ask the Boltons? As usual, compare these answers with your own. Now choose a partner and look at his or her answers. Then report back the results of your two questionnaires to the class.

When all the information has been returned, try and answer the following questions:

— How many families go abroad?
— What are the favourite destinations?
— What are the favourite holiday-spots in England?
— What do people enjoy doing most?

Look at this map of the British Isles. Using the information the class has collected, fill in the most visited areas and the activities they are popular for:

BRIGHTON
(5 Families in 10)
Swimming,
Sunbathing

Things to do

◊ Buy ten picture post-cards of the area in which you are living.

◊ If possible, buy a stick of rock (you can eat it or take it back as a souvenir).

◊ Write to your parents and suggest a plan for a touring holiday of England.

◊ Tell your host family some interesting places to visit in your home country.

◊ Go into a travel agency and ask for a brochure about holidays in England.

Eating Out

More and more people are eating out in England. Many pubs now serve hot food, ethnic restaurants have become extremely popular and every day a new fast food outlet opens.

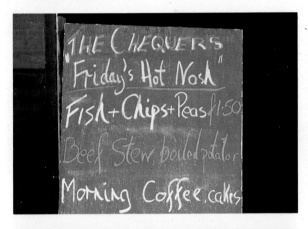

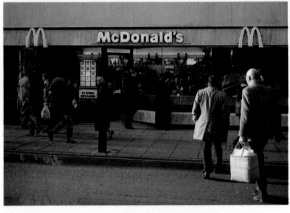

Look at these signs. In what sort of establishment would you expect to find them? What do they offer?

Ploughman's Lunch £1·20

Table D'Hôte Menu £6

Today's Special: Roast Beef & 2 Veg £3

Bombay Special Dinner £5

 Full Breakfast £4

Linklist

The subject of this Linklist is eating out and the kinds of food available in restaurants. Add to it as usual.

In Britain . . .	In my country . . .
◊ A lot of restaurants offer 'foreign' food.	◊
◊ People eat out on special occasions like birthdays.	◊
◊ Cafés are cheaper and simpler than restaurants. They rarely serve alcohol.	◊
◊ A lot of pubs now serve good, cheap food.	◊
◊	◊
◊	◊
◊	◊
◊	◊
◊	◊
◊	

Groupwork

Ask someone in your class:

◊ Have you eaten in a restaurant or café in England? What kind? What were your impressions?

◊ What are ethnic restaurants?

◊ Are there any restaurants in this town serving food from your country?

◊ How do prices compare with those in your country? Do you think eating out is expensive here?

With a partner, look at the following menu. The café owner has asked you to put the menu up on the 'Today's Special' board. He has given you the names of the dishes but they are mixed up. Put the names together, then put the dishes under the correct headings:

		STARTERS	MAIN DISHES	EXTRAS
Prawn	rabbit			
Fish and	toast			
Sausages and	cocktail			
Beans on	mash			
Welsh	chips			
Bacon and	pie			
Shepherd's	eggs			
Egg	cream			
Fruit and	mayonnaise			
Bread and	custard			
Apple pie and	butter			
Fruit	soup			
Vegetable	juice			

With the same partner, imagine you are going to set up a 'typically English' restaurant in your own country.

What would you call it?

Where would it be?

What would it serve?

You have to organise an evening out for a group of people. Here are the selections:

TRADITIONAL ENGLISH FAYRE

★ Brown Windsor Soup
★ Roast Beef &
   Yorkshire pudding
★ Sherry trifle
★ Cheese and celery

£15

BALI BANQUET

Sweet & sour shrimp
Spicy octopus
Chicken curry & rice
Lady's fingers
Exotic fruit salad

£18

FAST FOOD

★ Special
      cheeseburger
★ Onion rings
★ French fries
★ Apple pie/cream

£3

CHEZ PIERRE

Snails in garlic
Frogs' legs
Lamb's brains
Cheeses
Chocolate mousse

£24 without wine

JOE'S FISH BAR

Shrimp cocktail
Deep-fried cod
  with chips & peas
Bread & butter
Ice cream

£5.60

Choose a sixth possibility which would please *you*. Perhaps it could be typical of your country. The people in the group are:—

Colonel Smythe Ex-Indian Army; loves curries but hates 'foreign' food.

Mrs Healey Likes anything simple but *not* hamburgers.

Paul and Carole King Young, trendy couple; like anything new and chic.

Avon Pearce Food critic; very difficult; looking for good value.

John and Sheila Winters He's on a limited budget, she's on a diet. Be careful!

Jean-Pierre Schmidt In England for the first time; wants to try local food.

With a partner, try and choose one menu that will please everybody. If you can't find one, make one up yourselves.

Words

Check that you understand this vocabulary.

You can eat in a restaurant/a pub/a café/a fish-and-chip shop/a fast food place.

You can order a set meal/à la carte/today's special/a snack.

You may have a choice of several courses: a starter/a main dish/a sweet/a dessert/a pudding.

Check that the prices are all-inclusive. This means they include service/VAT/ cover charge. You may want to leave a tip for the waiter/waitress.

At the end of the meal you ask for the bill.
If the establishment is unlicensed, you cannot buy alcohol.

Write down any extra vocabulary below:

Listening

If you have time, listen to what these people have to say about 'Eating Out'.

◊ Mr Davidson, Manager, Hamburger Chain _____

◊ Mr Simons, Owner and Chef, The Robin Hood _____

◊ Mr Marshall, Publican _____

◊ Mrs Belaney, aged 27 _____

◊ Mr Duncan, aged 45 _____

Out

Ready?
In today's Enquiry, we are going to do two things:

— make a survey of restaurants, pubs and cafés in your town.
— organise a lunch or dinner for the class or for your host family.

Steady . . .

For the survey, you should choose a section of the town which has several eating places and divide up the different places into categories according to price. For example, a meal for under £3, a meal for under £6 and — luxury! — a meal for £10 or more. You will also have to agree on what a meal includes (how many courses? drinks included? etc.).

Look at this information sheet.

£	NAME & ADDRESS	TYPE	FOOD	DRINKS	SERVICE	ENTERTAINMENT
3	The Black Bear 41, High St	PUB	Sandwiches, Salad, Sausages	Beer, Wine by the glass	at the bar	juke-box, darts
	McDan's 36 New St	FAST FOOD	Burgers, French fries	Coke, Milk Shakes	Self-service	none
6	Taj Mahal 9 Cross St	INDIAN	Curries; Some English dishes	No licence	waiter	none
	Fok Lo 16 New St	CHINESE	Mandarin; some English dishes	Beer	waiter	none
10+	L'Escargot 13 Castle St	FRENCH	Classic French Cuisine (£15+)	Licensed	waiter	none
	The Cheshire Cheese 8 Lower St	ENGLISH	Roasts, pies etc.	Licensed	waiter	none

Divide into groups. Each group should work on one category.

Go!

Let's go. Remember, there are special laws about places serving alcohol.
Look at this sign. What do you think it means?

Feedback

Using the information you have collected, decide whether you wish to organise a class meal or a thank-you meal for your host family.

You will need to answer a list of questions before deciding on a place. Here are some suggestions. You can ask your class-mates directly, but you will have to use tact and discretion if you are going to invite your family . . .

TASTE: — What kind of food? Does everyone agree?
     — What kind of restaurant would suit a special occasion?

BUDGET: — How much can you afford?
     — Do the prices include service and VAT?
     — What is the average cost per person?

CONDITIONS: — Are there any legal restrictions (licensing laws)?
     — Where is the restaurant? How will you travel?
     — Do they accept travellers' cheques/credit cards/ Eurocheques?
     — Can you do the washing up if you don't have enough money?
     — Are there any dress requirements (no jeans, collar and tie)?

You see? It is not as simple as that! Make up your own list of questions and write them down together with the answers. When you have decided where to go, find the telephone number, call the restaurant and reserve a table.

Things to do

◊ Try and find a traditional English restaurant. (It is not always easy!) Copy down part of the menu and the prices.

◊ Look for a restaurant serving your national food. Is it authentic? Why? Why not? What is missing?

◊ What exactly are the licensing laws? Are there any historical reasons for them? What do English people think of them?

◊ Phone a restaurant in which you would like to eat. Ask them about opening/closing times, dress requirements etc.

Leisure

 Here are some of the ways in which English people spend their free time. Do you know any of the games that they play? What other sports and games are popular? Does anyone in your host family play a sport?

What are these objects connected with?

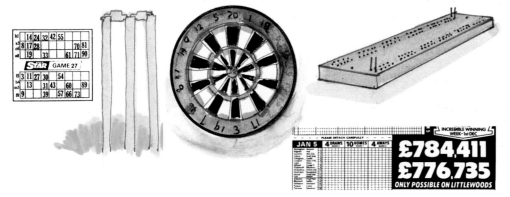

_____

_____

_____

_____

_____

Let's look at the Entertainment section in the local paper and see what's on in town. Look at the advertisements and notices in the paper or the ones below:

What facilities are available in your town for an evening out? Write them down.

_____

_____

_____

_____

Linklist

The subject of this Linklist is games and other leisure activities and how people spend their free time. Add to it as usual.

In Britain . . .	In my country . . .
◊ The most popular sport is football.	◊
◊ There are many public sports facilities.	◊
◊ A lot of people go to evening classes, especially in winter.	◊
◊ The favourite evening activity is watching TV.	◊
◊ Many homes have video recorders.	◊
◊	◊
◊	◊
◊	◊
◊	◊
◊	◊
◊	◊

Groupwork

Let's all go out for the evening! Here are some special packages offered by London Tours Ltd. Look at them and see which you prefer:

THEATRELAND ★ Visit backstage of a famous theatre ★ See 'The Mousetrap' and meet the actors ★ Souvenir programme £15 each	THAMES CRUISE Guided night tour on the Thames to see London by night. Dinner on board £30 each	**1930s EVENING** ● Dinner and dancing at the Savoy ● Top hat and tails £63 each
PUNK TOUR *See London's punks Visit a famous punk club and do the Pogo all night Costume provided Hamburgers at McDonalds* *£6 each*	**WALKING TOUR** ★ Visit unknown London on foot ★ Soho, Chinatown and the back-streets ★ Dinner in a Chinese restaurant £22 each	

Which of these would you choose? It's more difficult if it is a group decision! Discuss which package your group would choose, or, better still, plan your own evening out.

Words

Check that you understand this vocabulary.

to spend your free time/leisure time at the cinema/playing tennis/taking photographs.

Collecting stamps, posters and records, making models, and keeping pets are all common hobbies among children.

Football, golf, cricket, boxing are all popular spectator sports.

People of all ages take part in sports — they want to be energetic/active/to get fit.

Write down any extra vocabulary below:

Listening

If you have time, listen to what these people have to say about 'Leisure'.

◊ Mr Dowd, Manager, Odeon Multi-Screen _____

◊ Mr Maclaren, aged 38 _____

◊ President of a sports club _____

◊ A sports reporter _____

Out

Ready?
Let's ask your host family about their leisure interests.
Divide into groups of three. Discuss in your groups what questions you are going to ask. Make a provisional list.

Steady . . .
Report back to the class. The class will decide on the final list together. Copy it down.

Go!

`'May I ask you a few questions, please?'`

MINI-POLL

i   Do you spend most of your leisure time *(a)* at home? *(b)* outside?

ii Do you go to the cinema *(a)* once a month? *(b)* more often? (say how often). *(c)* less often? (say how often).

iii What do you do in your spare time? *(a)* Go to restaurants? *(b)* Go dancing. *(c)* Go to the cinema or theatre. *(d)* Something else.

iv When you are at home with the family, do you *(a)* watch TV? *(b)* play video games? *(c)* read? *(d)* do something else?

v   Do you ever *(a)* play bingo? *(b)* bet on horse races? *(c)* do the football pools?

Now you carry on . . .

_____

_____

_____

_____

_____

_____

_____

_____

Feedback

Here are the answers given by Mr and Mrs Headcote in Poole:

1 We spend most of our time indoors, watching television.
2 We go out for a meal about twice a year for special occasions.
3 We often invite friends around for drinks and dinner.
4 My husband plays football with the local team on Sunday.
5 We have done the pools for the last ten years without winning.
6 We don't go to the cinema much now because we have a video recorder.
7 We sometimes go dancing at the Mecca.
8 We only go to the theatre if we visit London.
9 My wife belongs to a social club.
10 At Christmas, we have a family party and play games.

Choose a partner and compare answers with him or her. Then compare both your sets of answers with other pairs. Finally, pool information on the board, like this:

LEISURE SURVEY

	Put a mark for each activity mentioned	TOTAL
HOME-BASED ACTIVITIES ◊ Gardening		
◊ Watching TV		
◊		
◊		
SPORTING ACTIVITIES ◊ Swimming		
◊ Football		
◊		
◊		
OUTSIDE ACTIVITIES ◊ Going to the cinema		
◊ Going for a meal		
◊		
◊		

NUMBER OF PEOPLE INTERVIEWED: _____

FAVOURITE HOME-BASED ACTIVITY: _____

FAVOURITE SPORTING ACTIVITY: _____

FAVOURITE OUTSIDE ACTIVITY: _____

Then write a short paragraph on what the survey tells you about British people and their leisure time.

_____

_____

_____

_____

_____

_____

_____

_____

_____

Things to do

◊ Find an English MONOPOLY set and see how it differs from Monopoly in your country.

◊ Ask someone to explain the rules of cricket to you — when you have understood, write to your English teacher at home with a detailed description.

◊ Explain your favourite game to your host family. Do they know it?

◊ Start a collection of cinema tickets, theatre tickets, etc. to remind you of your time in England.

People

 Here are some of the faces you may see during your stay here. Who are they? Where would you see them? Who is the missing figure? You fill it in.

79

Linklist

Our last Linklist is slightly different. In the centre, there is a list of people you find in most countries. Fill in what each is like in your country. Then, in the right hand column, put your impressions of what they are like in Britain. If you haven't met them, think of what you have seen or read here. Add others you have met.

In my country . . .	People	In Britain . . .
	bus driver	
rather severe and distant; dull uniform	policeman	friendly and helpful; funny hat !
	soldier on guard	
	butcher or baker	
	businessman	
	politician	
	doctor / nurse	
	student	
	waiter / waitress	

Groupwork

Madame Tussaud was born in France two hundred years ago but became famous in England because she made wax figures and opened a gallery which still exists today. There are famous people from the past and the present. There is also a Chamber of Horrors full of murderers and other unpleasant people. Brr!

Imagine that Madame Tussaud's has asked you and a partner to open a special British gallery which represents aspects of Britain. Who would you put in? (Think of sports personalities, TV stars, musicians, . . .). Choose as many as you like. Compare your list with those of the other pairs.

Finally, as a class, make up a list of 15 people.

_____

_____

_____

_____

_____

_____

_____

_____

Words

Check that you understand this vocabulary.

To describe people physically:
tall   thin (slim)   fat (plump)   old (elderly) _____

To describe people's characters:
patient   generous   kind   reserved   selfish _____

the most/least enjoyable thing about Britain is _____

to be pleasantly surprised by (the way people) _____

to disapprove of (the way people) _____

Talk about people's attitudes/behaviour/opinions

Write down any extra vocabulary below:

Listening

If you have time, listen to what these people have to say about 'People'.

◊ Mrs Taylor, aged 28 _____

◊ A Senior Citizen _____

◊ Tom Radcliffe, aged 38 _____

◊ A Bus Conductor _____

Out

Ready?

This is called an 'Identikit' picture. It is made up of separate parts — eyes, ears, hair-styles, noses and so on. They are combined to form a complete picture.

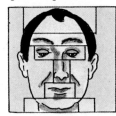

Steady . . .

We are going to try and do this for the British — not a physical portrait, though. We want a picture of their character — or characters.

Go!

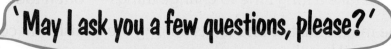

'May I ask you a few questions, please?'

MINI-POLL

i   Are the British *(a)* welcoming? *(b)* distant and reserved? *(c)* the same as anyone else?

ii   Do you feel you are *(a)* English/Scottish/Welsh/Irish? *(b)* British? *(c)* European? *(d)* All three?

iii   Which phrase sums up the British best? *(a)* 'A nice cup of tea' *(b)* 'God save the Queen' *(c)* 'Please queue here'.

iv   Which sentence sums up Britain's attitude to foreign tourists? *(a)* They bring in a lot of money. *(b)* They spoil our cities. *(c)* It is a compliment that people want to visit Britain.

v   Do you *(a)* always buy British goods? *(b)* choose the best value product from whatever country? *(c)* try to buy goods from a particular country?

vi   Are young people today *(a)* proud to be British? *(b)* happy to be British? *(c)* indifferent? *(d)* like young people everywhere?

Now you carry on . . .

_____

_____

_____

_____

_____

Feedback

Here are the answers of Mr and Mrs Parkinson in Cambridge:

1 The British are very reserved but they are friendly.
2 We — the English — are a little suspicious of foreigners.
3 We feel proud to be British but our son doesn't care.
4 Symbols of England? The Union Jack, Nelson's Column and bangers.
5 I didn't realise we *were* in the Common Market.
6 We travel abroad for our holidays; we have been to 4 other countries.
7 At home we would miss things like French wine, Italian coffee, German beer and Dutch chocolate.
8 Younger English people are more open in their attitudes than their parents.
9 I feel very free here; there are no identity cards.
10 The British take a long time to change things — often too long.

What are the main qualities and faults among the British that come out of the class information? List them.

_____

_____

_____

_____

_____

Now, find a partner (of the same nationality as you, if possible) and ask him or her the same questions as above — but about *your* country.

Quiz

Divide into 2 teams then work out a list of questions which will test how much you have all used your eyes and ears while you have been in Britain. Here are some suggestions:

What do the yellow lines painted on the roads mean?
Who is the leader of the Opposition?
What does 'fare stage' on a bus stop mean?
Where would you see a TO LET sign? What does it mean?
Which football team is top of Division I?
Which TV channels have no advertising?
Where is Stonehenge?
Which record is Number 1 in the Hit Parade?
What can you buy at Boots?

Now you carry on . . .

_____

_____

_____

_____

The two teams sit facing each other. Ask the person opposite you a question. Two points if he or she answers it correctly and without help. If they do not know the answer, anyone on the team may reply for one point.

When everyone in your team has asked a question, it is your opponents' turn.

The losing team has to come back to Britain again. And although the winning team are experts, they should return from time to time to keep their knowledge up to date!

See you soon!

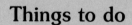

Things to do

◊ Find out the significance of the Union Jack, then design a new British flag.

◊ Look at the words to 'God save the Queen'.

◊ Find out more about Madame Tussaud's — or, better still, visit her gallery.

◊ Start planning your next visit!

Teaching notes

These notes should be read in conjunction with the Introduction at the beginning of the book.

Streetwork
This section introduces the language the students will need when asking questions in the street, and at home if they are living with a host family.
The teacher may find it useful to return to this section several times for further practice in the early stages of the course.

Tipsheets
This section is designed to be completed by individual students for their own reference.
It should be read through in class during the first week of the course and points arising discussed. Students should be encouraged to enlist the help of the host family in completing it where possible. Information can also be exchanged among students in class.

Tapescripts
The words of the song, 'Let's investigate . . .' — written specially for this course, and the Listening sections from the ten topics are printed in full after these Teaching notes. Students should be encouraged to listen to the song and the Listening sections without looking at the script initially, but the scripts can be used for further discussion and language practice later.

Topics
Each topic is divided into three parts, **In, Out** and **Feedback.**
In contains classroom activities to think about, discuss and prepare.
Out includes preparation of the Enquiry or Mini-poll, which are completed outside the classroom.
Feedback pools and examines the results of the Enquiry or Mini-poll.
The time taken to cover each topic will vary from centre to centre but will usually take two or three days to complete even when working fairly intensively with the course. Some teachers, however, may prefer to allow students more time to carry out their investigations or run two topics in parallel in the same week.

NB Remember that the order of the topics may be changed to take into account the interests of each group.

In contains the introductory text and picture-based vocabulary exercises.
The Linklist is designed to make the students think about their own country and compare it with what they know and find out — individually and as a group — about the same areas of British life. Information is gathered from the teacher, from classmates and outside the classroom and the Linklist is completed. It can be set as homework for the following day's classes or completed at the end of the topic.
Groupwork includes practice exercises to be done in small groups of two, three or four.
The instructions in the book are kept deliberately spare. The tasks may be simplified or made more complex, depending on the level and interests of the group.
The Listening section is designed for use with higher level groups as a basis for further vocabulary and discussion work. The sections can be used with lower levels groups, but the teacher may wish to introduce and pre-teach some of the words and expressions used. (See Tapescript.)

Out contains practice and preparation for the Enquiry or Mini-poll. The Enquiry involves students in observation while the Mini-poll involves them in asking questions and seeking information by asking questions.
Both activities allow participation by students of varying levels. The Mini-poll obliges students to write their own questions in advance. Questions can be open-ended or multiple choice allowing both stronger and weaker students to formulate questions at the appropriate level.
Since the students will be obliged to come into daily contact with British people, a certain amount of tact will be necessary. A careful study and practice of the material contained in Streetwork should avoid embarrassment on both sides. (See, also, 'A final word for teachers' in the Introduction.)

NB **Always** make sure that younger students interview strangers in groups, **never** alone.

Feedback is the pooling and analysis of the information gathered. Encourage students to concentrate on gathering information about what British people do, think and feel rather than pass judgements. 'Things to do' is designed to suggest interesting and fun things for students to do while they are in the country. Students can select for themselves which suggestions to follow up, or suggest their own further activities. And once teachers get to know the class, they can suggest things to do which take into account the age and interests of the students and what the local community has to offer of interest to them.

Supplementary materials
Teachers will find it useful to keep a supply of supplementary materials in the classroom to use in conjunction with the coursebook. Below is a list of suggested sources to accompany each topic. Space is also left for teachers to add their own ideas when preparing their lessons.
We hope both teachers and students enjoy using **Investigations** as much as did groups who used it in the trialling version.

Homes
Home magazines
Estate agents' blurbs
DIY magazines
Local newspaper
Town map with street index

Towns
Local information leaflets
Timetables
Town map
Local newspapers
Information about twin towns

Television
Radio Times
TV Times
Newspaper programme guide
TV licence
Books based on popular TV series

Shopping
Town map
Ads for local shops
Special offer coupons

Meals
English cookery book or recipes
Cans etc. of popular foods (or labels)

Travelling
Local timetables
Highway code
Selection of travel tickets
Local Ordnance Survey map

Holidays
Holiday brochures for British resorts
AA Guide to Britain
Map of Britain

Eating Out
Local takeaway restaurant menus
Local paper

Leisure
Local paper
Sports centre leaflets
Bingo cards
Games (cards, backgammon etc.)

People
Madame Tussaud's brochure

Tapescripts

The song 'Let's Investigate' is recorded at the beginning of Side 1 and Side 2 of the cassette.

Song: Let's Investigate . . .

Verse Talk about the people you have seen,
And the places you have been,
Start to ask the questions in your mind,
And the answers you will find.

Chorus *Let's investigate,*
Investigate,
Let's investigate,
What we see and do,
Let's investigate,
Investigate,
Let's investigate,
All we see and do.

Verse Reaching out to learn new things is fun,
Making notes of what you've done,
What is strange and what's the same,
Let's investigate — our game.

Chorus

Instrumental

Chorus to fade

Words and Music by Duncan Lorien © 1984

Homes

A Councillor

◊ There aren't enough Council-houses. Waiting lists are huge: it can take 3 to 5 years to get a place. The Government should spend more, build more housing estates. There's a terrible housing shortage in this city.

Mr Williams   Aged 32

◊ When we got married, we moved into a rented bungalow. We saved up enough money with the Building Society to buy a terraced house. We've had to do a lot of work on it, but it is ours. Now we want to sell it and move out to the suburbs. Yes, I want the kids to be able to play outside without worrying about the traffic.

An Architect

◊ I know people say that all English houses look the same, but that's just on the outside. Inside, each house is very different. Each one reflects the people who live there. You know what they say: an Englishman's home is his castle. Well, it's true. People spend a lot of time and money to make their homes comfortable.

An Estate Agent

◊ This is a beautiful home. Excellent value. It has two reception rooms, a kitchen and a toilet downstairs. There is a master bedroom and two smaller rooms upstairs with a bathroom and a separate toilet. It is close to the shops and all major bus-routes. The lease-hold price is just £35,000. A real bargain at today's inflated prices.

Towns

A Newcomer

◊ It's great to be in a small place after years of living in a city. People talk to you here. I live 10 minutes' walk from work and, although the bus service could be better, it's easy to get around. There's more time for things like clubs and evening classes — and walking in the park.

Peter Hanson   Aged 17

◊ We've always lived here. My father works in the local factory but I've been unemployed since I left school. Some of my friends have moved to London. Not me, though — it's cheaper to live at home and I'd miss the football.

A Local Businessman

◊ What we need is a ring road to cut down the traffic through the middle of town — make it safer for people to walk around. And cheaper car parking, as well, to encourage more shoppers. My company gives money to local charities and we provide a lot of jobs. When is the council going to help us?

Harold Clark   Aged 73

◊ I love it here. I've got a free bus pass and I go into the town centre most days — I read the newspapers in the library and walk round the shops. The council have made a real effort in my area — more trees and flowers, more litter bins, and a day centre for Senior Citizens like me.

Television

A Primary School Teacher

◊ The kids in my class have all got square eyes! They get home at four thirty and CLICK they turn on the box. Parents have no control and some of the programmes are really violent. It's their responsibility to teach their kids to appreciate the television and not to watch just anything. There are terrible problems with reading and writing. Kids don't read books any more, they just turn on the telly.

A Secondary School Pupil   Aged 12

◊ Television is a great way to learn. It teaches you about subjects you normally wouldn't learn about. It's easier than reading a book and it's more realistic, more up-to-date. I wish we could watch more television in schools.

A Politician

◊ British television is the best in the world. We have variety and quality. We try to entertain and educate. In no other country in the world do you find this policy. That is why so many British television programmes are exported. We need more channels and more broadcasting. Up to 20 hours a day for example.

A Young Viewer

◊ Most telly programmes are rubbish. Too serious. I wish there were more police shows and sports. And more adverts too. Television should be entertainment; you know, fun. The telly in Britain isn't as good as in America. I wish they'd bring back Starsky and Hutch. I watch about five hours a day.

Shopping

A Shopkeeper

◊ The Government should change the laws about opening and closing times. We should be allowed to stay open later and close in the afternoons. We've got lazy. If you want to buy a packet of washing powder at seven in the evening, you can't. In most families, both husband and wife work. It would be doing everyone a favour. And as for the Sunday opening laws, they're ridiculous.

A Lady Shopper

◊ I much prefer supermarkets and shopping centres. The little corner shops were nice but they were too small and expensive. At least in a supermarket you can find everything you need under one roof. We have to move with the times.

A Department Store Manager

◊ We have a terrible problem with shop-lifting. You know, it's difficult to control because of staff problems. People want to take their time, choose what they want from the shelves — but we need tighter security because often the customer 'forgets' to pay. We've tried everything — security guards, electronic alarms — you name it. The only solution is higher prices to cover our losses. It's the only way.

A Sub-Post Mistress   Aged 67

◊ My husband and I, we used to run a sub-post office and village store. The GPO closed down the post office and we couldn't afford to compete against those big chain-stores. We knew all of our customers; it was a real service that we provided, but what can you do? The way of life has changed.

Meals

A Businessman

◊ Food's not important to me. I only eat when I'm hungry — just a snack, though — I haven't got time for proper meals. The only meal I really look forward to is Sunday lunch. We always have a roast and a proper pudding.

A Teacher

◊ It's easy to get into bad habits about food when you live alone. You tend to live on sandwiches and cups of coffee. I try to eat a hot meal every day, even if it's only baked beans. I don't really plan meals. I just eat whatever's in the fridge.

A Northerner Living in the South

◊ When I first moved down South I got very confused about meals. At home we had breakfast, dinner and tea but here they call it breakfast, lunch and dinner. I still make mistakes sometimes.

Helen Jones   Aged 42

◊ Mealtimes are very important in this family. It's the only time we all get together. It's not formal — just a chance to talk and listen to each other. The children know they have to be there and no television is allowed!

Travelling

A Bus Driver

◊ Things are better now — I mean more efficient. Most routes are pay-as-you-enter. You know, no more conductors. But queues are longer — and the traffic! O.K., we've got more bus lanes but traffic in the city centre is still awful. We need more pedestrian areas. Only people who work in the centre should be allowed to drive their cars in town. It's a difficult job, driving a bus.

A Passenger

◊ The service is worse these days. Fewer buses and longer waits. These one-man buses are no answer. And fares get higher and higher. Funny, isn't it? There are fewer people but it costs more. There are bus passes for senior citizens and what-have-you but, still, 95 pence to go into town is a lot of money.

A Councillor

◊ The Council is considering banning cars from the city centre. We'll build a huge car park and operate shuttle buses into the centre. It's more expensive initially but life will be easier for the motorist and for bus drivers.

A Member of a Watchdog Committee

◊ The London Underground — you know, the Tube — is out-of-date and over-priced. The rolling stock — the trains and so on — are old and badly designed. We need to modernise them and to introduce a flat-fare system like in other countries. It will cost a lot of money, but the ratepayer will be better-off in the end.

Holidays

Mrs Rodgers   Aged 47

◊ We never go abroad. England's good enough for us. Why go to other countries when you don't know your own? I've no time for these package holidays on the Mediterranean. No, we choose a nice seaside resort like Clacton or Skegness and off we go. Three weeks in a bed-and-breakfast makes a real break.

Malcolm D'Arcy   Aged 32

◊ My wife and I usually go to France for the hols. Either to the Alps for the ski-ing or to the Dordogne. If you choose your spot correctly, you always have other English people around you. You can even get a decent cup of tea.

A Travel Agent

◊ We've noticed that more and more people of all ages want to travel abroad nowadays. Our agency organises trips for all sorts of different groups: over-65s, under 20s, cyclists, honeymooners — even rock-climbers. Spain's the most popular destination, followed by France. Prices are going down because of the numbers and low air-fares. We sometimes have problems with local hotels but things usually go well.

Diego Vergara

◊ I live in Torremolinos and I don't like the English. They come here, they want everything just like in England. They never try to speak Spanish, or to meet the people. They have parties, they drink too much and then there's trouble. I say: English go home!

Eating Out

Mr Davidson, Manager, Hamburger Chain

◊ The whole idea of eating out is changing. People today want to eat nourishing food at a reasonable cost with no fuss or wasted time. The old restaurants are on their way out. The long lunch hour is a thing of the past. The micro-wave and the hamburger are the future. People will have more time to do what they want.

Mr Simons, Owner and Chef, The Robin Hood

◊ I was going to open a French restaurant but my wife said: There's 3 French restaurants in town already. Why not open an English one? So we did. We serve all the traditional food — pies, puddings, fools and whatnot. We find recipes in old books and try them out. There's a new interest in English food — but mainly among American tourists!

Mr Marshall, Publican

◊ Pubs used to be associated with beer, with sandwiches or rolls to eat and maybe a bit of pie or cheese from time to time. Today we sell more and more food — and people actually come to pubs to eat out. Quality has got better. Above all, the food's more imaginative. And our profits have gone up considerably. In fact, it's food we make our money on now, not drink.

Mrs Belaney   Aged 27

◊ We don't eat out often. Maybe at the weekend, we'll go to an Indian or Chinese because it's cheap and good quality. Or we may have a take-away if I'm too tired to cook. On a special occasion, like our anniversary, we'll treat ourselves and go to the good Italian or French restaurants in town. But not often because it's so expensive. We need cafés like they have on the Continent.

Mr Duncan   Aged 45

◊ We'd rather go out for a meal than go to the cinema or theatre. We've got several favourites. We look for peace and quiet, good service, fresh food and something extra — a good view or live music perhaps.

Leisure

Mr Dowd, Manager, Odeon Multi-Screen

◊ This used to be a big cinema with just one screen and 2 films at every showing. Now, to survive, we've divided the building up into 4 separate cinemas each showing a different film. There's so much competition from the TV and videos that, if we don't find new ideas soon, we'll all have to close.

Mr Maclaren   Aged 38

◊ I don't spend much, but I bet regularly: football pools, the dogs, the horses, that sort of thing. I don't take it too seriously. I suppose I spend a tenner a week, sometimes more. And I get the odd win now and again. I got this year's Derby winner — 250 quid.

President, Sports Club

◊ Ladies and Gentlemen, the Club has had an excellent year. Our soccer and rugby teams are at the top of their respective divisions; in tennis, squash and badminton, our players have won 15 trophies. Mike Delaney has won the Open Golf Championship and our rowing crews are doing wonderfully. In fencing and archery we've been a little weaker, but not to worry. Our problem now is to find a new sport to include in next year's programme!

A Sports Reporter

◊ A report just published today shows that the favourite leisure activity in England today is . . . watching television. Next comes watching sports. Are the English lazy? On the Continent people play more sport than over here. All we're famous for now is the bad behaviour of our football supporters. Come on England! Play the ball!

People

Mrs Taylor   Aged 28

◊ Being British means being part of a mixed community. My son's class at school includes West Indian children, Chinese, Spanish, Pakistani . . . I think it's marvellous — it helps them understand different cultures, different religions, clothes, food, languages.

A Senior Citizen

◊ People have no manners today. They don't queue for buses any more. You see young kids dropping litter and playing loud radios in the street. No-one cares.

Tom Radcliffe   Aged 38

◊ I never read the gossip columns. I'm not interested in what rock stars or sportsmen or the royal family are up to. They're entitled to their private life like anyone else.

A Bus Conductor

◊ The summer's the most difficult time. All the foreign visitors trying to work out the money, not knowing where they're going. It's chaos.